Joachim and Anne had a beautiful baby girl whom they named Mary.

**Mary grew up in a town called Nazareth.
She went to school and learned many things.**

**Mary's parents taught her to love and obey God,
and this made her want to go and help others in need.**

When she was a young woman, an angel from God appeared to her, to bring her some special news.

**"You will have a baby boy and his name will be Jesus.
He will be God's son," he told her.**

"I am happy and willing to do whatever God asks of me," Mary answered.

**Mary ran to tell Joseph the good news.
Joseph was soon to be her husband**

A new law in the country told everyone to go the town that they were born in, to pay their taxes.

Joseph and Mary lived in Nazareth, but they had to travel to the town of Bethlehem, far far away.

Back in those days, they didn't have cars, trains or airplanes. So they walked and rode on a donkey.

It was difficult for Mary, because she was tired and soon ready to have her baby.

When they finally arrived in Bethlehem, it was crowded with people. All the hotels were full.

But Mary didn't worry. "I know that God will provide us with a place to stay." she said.

They finally stayed in an old barn. Not very warm and cozy. And not very fancy for a king to be born in.

But Mary didn't complain. "This must be God's will," she said. "And for that I am thankful."

**Having a baby was a new experience for Mary.
She learned many things about being a good mother to Jesus.**

But in everything that Mary did, she gave glory to God. "Baby dear, God loves us all, even these tiny birds!" she said.

**Joseph and Mary loved children.
They taught them to love and spend time with God.**

Joseph worked in his carpentry shop to provide for his family. Mary fed the children and took care of the home.

Every year the family would travel to the city of Jerusalem, to the temple, for a special time of praise and worship.

One day when Jesus was 12 years old, his parents looked for him for 3 days, until they finally found him talking to the elders of the temple.

As Jesus grew to be a man and began His special mission, Mary went along with Him, as one of His followers.

She even encouraged him to perform His first miracle, of changing the water to wine.

**Mary's heart filled with joy and trust in God.
Everything that God promised had come true.**

Get FREE downloads

Published by iCharacter Ltd. (Ireland)
www.icharacter.org
By Agnes and Salem de Bezenac
Illustrated by Agnes de Bezenac
Copyright 2015. All rights reserved.

Copyright © 2015 by iCharacter Ltd.. All rights reserved. No part of this book may be reproduced in any form or by any electronic or mechanical means, including information storage and retrieval systems, without written permission from the publisher or author, except in the case of a reviewer, who may quote brief passages embodied in critical articles or in a review.

www.ingramcontent.com/pod-product-compliance
Lightning Source LLC
Chambersburg PA
CBHW081504070526
44586CB00019B/2468